I0429776

A BUSINESS APPROACH TO GERANIUM FARMING

Complete Entrepreneurial Step By Step Guide To Geranium Garden From Scratch

ZHURI HART

DISCLAIMER

This book is intended to provide general information and insights on adopting a business approach to farming. The content within is based on the author's knowledge and experiences up to the date of publication. It is essential to recognize that the field of agriculture is dynamic, influenced by various factors such as market conditions, climate, and regulatory changes.

Readers are advised to conduct thorough research, seek professional advice, and consider their unique circumstances before implementing any strategies or practices discussed in this book. The author and publisher disclaim any responsibility for the accuracy, completeness, or suitability of the information provided. The book is not a substitute for professional advice, and the author and publisher shall not be liable for any damages or losses arising from the use or reliance on the information presented herein.

Individual results may vary, and success in farming enterprises is contingent upon numerous variables. The author encourages readers to consult with relevant experts, agricultural extension services, and legal or financial professionals to tailor strategies to their specific needs and local conditions.

This book is not intended to be a comprehensive guide to all aspects of farming, and readers should exercise their judgment and discretion in applying the principles discussed. The author and publisher do not endorse any specific products, services, or companies mentioned in this book unless explicitly stated.

By reading this book, the reader acknowledges and accepts the inherent uncertainties in agricultural endeavors and agrees to use the information at their own risk.

TABLE OF CONTENTS

ABOUT THE BOOK

The thorough manual "A Business Approach to Geranium Farming" explores the nuances of geranium production from a business standpoint. This book is important because it provides geranium farmers, both new and experienced, with the information and tactics they need to launch and run a profitable business in the geranium sector.

Setting the scene, the introduction gives an outline of geranium cultivation, explains the goal of the book, and gives some background information on geranium farming. Readers should take note of this preparatory material since it sets the stage for the next chapters and clarifies the significance of geraniums in the agriculture industry.

The book walks readers through the subtleties of geraniums, including their varieties, needs for soil and temperature, planting strategies, and ways to control pests and diseases. For farmers looking to maximize their geranium yields and quality and set themselves up for success in the cutthroat market, this fundamental knowledge is essential.

Any successful business endeavor requires market research and analysis, which is covered in the third portion of the book. The book gives farmers the tools they need to make smart decisions that will improve their competitiveness and market positioning by offering insights into market trends, competition analysis, target customer identification, and demand for geranium goods.

The book's emphasis on creating a solid business strategy is one of its strongest points. In this section, readers will get guidance on creating a vision and mission, establishing goals and objectives, taking legal considerations and laws into account, and doing risk assessments. Any geranium farming endeavor that hopes to succeed in the long run needs to have a well-organized business plan.

The technical aspects of geranium farming are covered in detail in the following sections. These include best practices for cultivation, farm setup, and harvesting. The book guarantees a comprehensive approach to geranium farming by providing insights into quality control and assurance, marketing and sales strategies, financial management, and sustainable practices. This covers every aspect required for a successful business.

The book tackles concerns that are frequently seen in the geranium farming sector and offers workable answers, making it an invaluable tool for resolving problems that can come up throughout the cultivation and company administration procedures. All things considered, "A Business Approach to Geranium Farming" serves as a thorough manual that meets the demands of both beginning and seasoned farmers, eventually promoting the expansion and sustainability of the geranium farming sector.

CHAPTER ONE

GERANIUM FARMING INTRODUCTION

BACKGROUND

Because these flowering plants are so distinctive and colorful, geranium farming has become very popular. This horticultural endeavor entails growing geraniums, which are prized for their adaptability and decorative appeal. This thorough introduction will cover a wide range of topics related to geranium farming, including understanding geraniums, investigating the various varieties, comprehending the soil and climate conditions that are unique to them, and going over the crucial procedures for planting and caring for geranium plants.

We will also discuss common pests and illnesses that geraniums can get, stressing the need for careful management to guarantee a healthy and eye-catching geranium garden.

SYNOPSIS OF GERANIUM PRODUCTION

Growing geraniums is a fulfilling hobby that blends artistic enjoyment with horticultural expertise. Members of the Pelargonium genus, geraniums are prized by both flower aficionados and gardeners for their unusual flowers and fragrant leaves. A variety of tasks are involved in farming, such as choosing appropriate cultivars, guaranteeing ideal growth circumstances, and resolving any obstacles. Geraniums are popular not only in traditional gardens but also in hanging baskets, container gardening, and even as houseplants, where they bring color and smell to a variety of environments.

KNOWING ABOUT GERANIUMS

A basic knowledge of the traits of the plant is essential for beginning geranium farming successfully. Geraniums are prized for both their varied foliage and flower forms, which range from traditional spherical blooms to more elaborate and lacy designs. The plant's overall appeal is enhanced by the leaves, which frequently have a unique scent. Geranium varieties come in a variety of growth patterns, including trailing, upright, and mounding, which opens up innovative landscaping possibilities. Understanding these subtleties empowers farmers and gardeners to make well-informed decisions about the choice and placement of geraniums in their landscapes.

DIFFERENT GERANIUM TYPES

A wide variety of species and cultivars, each with distinctive characteristics, are included in the geranium family. Zonen geraniums, ivy geraniums, regal geraniums, and scented-leaf geraniums are among the varieties that are frequently grown. Because of their strong growth and vivid colors, zonal geraniums—so named because of the distinct bands or zones on their leaves—are a popular choice. Ivy geraniums look great in hanging baskets and containers because of their trailing stems and cascading petals. Large, eye-catching blooms are the hallmark of regent geraniums, which are frequently used in elegant garden displays. Scent-leaf geraniums give off scents that range from citrus to rose, giving the garden an additional sensory element.

CONDITIONS OF THE SOIL AND CLIMATE

The provision of ideal environmental conditions is essential for geranium cultivation to succeed. Geraniums prefer mild weather, lots of sunshine, and soil that drains easily. Because they are frost-sensitive, these plants need to be protected over the winter. Sufficient ventilation and air movement are necessary to avoid common problems like fungal infections. To create an environment that supports the growth and development of geranium types, it is essential to understand the unique climate and soil preferences of each variety.

CARE AND PLANTING OF GERANIUMS

There are several factors to take into account while planting geranium plants, including soil preparation, time, and spacing. It's crucial to make sure that drainage and moisture retention are adequate when planting geraniums, whether they are in pots or on the ground. Geranium plants are generally healthier and live longer when they receive regular hydration, fertilization, and pruning. To maintain a healthy geranium garden, pest management methods, and disease prevention techniques are also essential. Farmers and gardeners can enjoy a continual display of vibrant blossoms throughout the growing season by following best practices in planting and care.

TYPICAL INSECTS AND ILLNESSES

Geraniums are resilient plants that can nonetheless be negatively impacted by several pests and diseases. Aphids, spider mites, and whiteflies are common pests that can be managed chemically or naturally. Certain environmental circumstances can lead to the occurrence of fungal diseases such as powdery mildew and botrytis, which highlights the significance of taking preventive measures and acting quickly.

By being aware of the symptoms of common pests and diseases, farmers can protect their geranium plants' health and attractiveness by putting efficient management techniques into place.

Geranium farming is a complex endeavor that includes appreciating a variety of species, comprehending particular cultivation needs, and resolving possible issues. Through exploring the nuances of geraniums—from kind and growth patterns to the preferred environment and maintenance requirements—farmers and gardeners can set out on a rewarding path to cultivating colorful and productive geranium gardens.

CHAPTER TWO

ANALYSIS AND RESEARCH ON THE MARKET

PRODUCT DEMAND FOR GERANIUM

Several factors, including increased consumer awareness of natural and organic components in personal care and wellness products, have contributed to the noticeable increase in demand for geranium products in recent years. The aromatherapy and cosmetics sectors have witnessed a surge in the popularity of geranium because of its unique fragrance and possible health advantages. Growing numbers of consumers are looking for products with natural ingredients; geranium, which is linked to relaxation and skincare, matches this trend.

Furthermore, the demand is increased by consumers who are health-conscious due to geranium's supposed antibacterial and anti-inflammatory qualities. Businesses in this sector need to stay aware of customer preferences to make sure that their products meet the changing demands of the market as demand for their products and services keeps rising.

OPPORTUNITIES & MARKET TRENDS

The market for geranium goods is being shaped by several trends, which offer businesses both opportunities and problems. The move toward eco-friendly and sustainable activities is one such trend. Nowadays, consumers are more likely to support companies that put environmental responsibility first. Businesses that sell geranium products can benefit from this trend by implementing eco-friendly packaging, transparent supply chains, and sustainable sourcing practices. The growth of digital platforms and e-commerce, which give companies a way to access a wider audience, is another noteworthy trend. Online shopping's ease has changed how people purchase, which presents many product producers with chances to improve their online visibility and interact with customers directly.

ANALYSIS OF COMPETITORS

To understand their position and pinpoint areas for improvement, companies in the geranium product industry must do a detailed competitor study. The product offerings, pricing schemes, distribution methods, and marketing techniques of rivals may differ. Businesses can improve their tactics and set themselves apart from the competition by evaluating the advantages and disadvantages of major rivals. To remain flexible in a changing market, it is essential to keep an eye on rival actions, such as the introduction of new products, advertising campaigns, and consumer feedback. Businesses can strategically position themselves by discovering market gaps to exploit or areas where they can flourish by acquiring insights into the competitive landscape.

DETERMINING THE TARGET MARKET

One of the most important first steps in creating geranium product marketing strategies is determining who your target market is. Businesses can better adapt their products and messaging to resonate with their target audience by having a thorough understanding of the psychographics, demographics, and behavior of potential customers. The target market for geranium goods may include people looking for organic and natural solutions for wellness and personal care. Analyzing consumer preferences and doing market research can yield important insights into the particular requirements and preferences of the target market. Furthermore, to enhance their targeting strategies, organizations had to take into account variables like purchasing habits, lifestyle preferences, and geographic location. Businesses can develop focused marketing campaigns and product offerings that appeal to their target audience by developing a precise and comprehensive profile of their target client.

CHAPTER THREE

CREATING A BUSINESS STRATEGY

MISSION AND VISION

The creation of a compelling vision and mission is essential to the formulation of a company plan. The vision, which outlines the long-term goals and main objective of the company, acts as a beacon. It outlines the company's future goals, motivating stakeholders and bringing everyone together under a single objective.

However, the mission statement explores the fundamental goals of the company, outlining its commitment to stakeholders, the reason for its existence, and the value it offers to clients.

In addition to offering guidance, these components serve as a basis for strategic decision-making, assisting the company in adhering to its mission and vision.

ESTABLISHING OBJECTIVES AND GOALS

Establishing clear goals and objectives is essential to a business strategy since it gives the organization a path forward for expansion and improvement. A goal is a broad, qualitative statement that describes the overall accomplishments that the company hopes to achieve. Conversely, objectives are more precise, quantifiable, and time-bound aims that help achieve those more general ones. The firm may improve focus, track progress, and make sure that efforts are focused on significant results by setting clear goals and objectives. Furthermore, to create a coherent strategy that advances the organization, these aims and objectives should be in line with its vision and mission.

REGULATIONS AND LEGAL ASPECTS

Making sense of the legal system is essential to creating a thorough business plan. Ensuring compliance and reducing potential hazards requires identifying and resolving legal considerations and laws pertinent to the industry and operation location. This entails being aware of what licenses, permits, and registrations the company needs to operate lawfully. It also necessitates an evaluation of potential legal difficulties, including those involving employment regulations, contracts, and intellectual property. A business strategy can proactively address compliance needs and lower the risk of legal difficulties that could obstruct the company's performance by incorporating a detailed review of legal considerations.

EVALUATION AND CONTROL OF RISKS

There are risks associated with every business endeavor, and a thorough business plan will contain a risk assessment and management approach. A crucial first step is identifying possible risks, whether they come from internal problems like operational inefficiencies or external ones like changes in the market. A risk management plan should be created when the hazards have been recognized and should include tactics for reducing, shifting, or accepting the risks. If hazards manifest, this plan should also include backup plans and procedures for handling emergencies. In addition to protecting the company, good risk management shows foresight and readiness, which inspires trust in partners, investors, and other stakeholders. The risk management plan's continued applicability as the business environment changes is ensured by routine reviews and updates.

CHAPTER FOUR

METHODS OF GROWING GERANIUMS

METHODS OF PROPAGATION

Several strategies are used in geranium farming to guarantee productive cultivation and ideal plant growth. The techniques used for propagation are essential to growing a robust geranium yield.

One popular method is seed propagation, which involves sowing geranium seeds in trays or seedbeds that have been properly prepared. For these seeds to germinate, they need a warm, humid atmosphere. Furthermore, stem cuttings are a widely used technique for propagating geraniums.

Through the process of root development stimulation and genetically identical plant production, producers can obtain healthy and disease-free cuttings from existing plants.

ROTATING CROPS AND PLANTING COMPANIONS

In geranium farming, crop rotation, and companion planting are crucial techniques for preserving soil fertility and preventing the accumulation of pests and diseases. By shifting the placement of geranium plants throughout the field every season, crop rotation helps to keep certain soil nutrients from being depleted. Growing geraniums next to other plants that complement each other well is known as companion planting. To improve crop health overall, growing geraniums with herbs like basil will help discourage certain pests.

WATER MANAGEMENT SYSTEMS

In geranium farming, irrigation systems are essential for providing the plants with enough water for growth and development. A popular technique, drip irrigation minimizes water waste and lowers the risk of diseases linked to overhead watering by delivering water directly to the plant roots.

It's critical to schedule irrigation properly, taking into account variables like soil composition, climate, and geranium plant growth stage.

ORGANIC AGRICULTURE METHODS

The growing demand for products cultivated organically has led to a rise in the popularity of geranium growth using organic farming methods. In organic geranium farming, natural substitutes for synthetic fertilizers and pesticides are used. In organic geranium farms, compost and well-rotted manure are frequently added to improve soil fertility. Furthermore, managing pests without the use of hazardous chemicals is made possible by natural pest management techniques like using neem oil or introducing helpful insects.

Cover cropping is a common technique used by organic geranium farmers to preserve soil health and stop nitrogen depletion. Legumes are examples of cover crops that may fix nitrogen in the soil, increasing its fertility. Moreover, mulching the soil organically using materials like wood chips or straw helps control soil temperature, weed suppression, and moisture retention.

Good propagation techniques, careful crop rotation and companion planting, excellent irrigation systems, and the use of organic farming methods are all necessary for successful geranium farming. Farmers may ensure high-quality yields while promoting sustainable geranium farming by putting these ideas into practice.

CHAPTER FIVE

HOW TO START A GERANIUM FARM

CHOOSING THE IDEAL SITE

The success of your geranium farm depends on where you decide to put it. Geraniums need lots of sunlight and well-drained soil to flourish. As such, choose a spot that receives full to partial sunshine all day long. Because geraniums are sensitive to wet circumstances, make sure the soil is well-aerated and rich in organic matter. Because geraniums have particular needs, take environment, temperature, and humidity into consideration. The optimal climate is usually mild, with temperatures between 60°F and 75°F. Strong wind protection is another way to keep the fragile geranium plants safe.

FARM DESIGN AND LAYOUT

Your geranium farm's layout and design are crucial for making the most use of available space, guaranteeing smooth operations, and fostering plant health. Arrange the beds or rows such that planting, watering, and harvesting may be done with ease. Make use of a layout that maximizes sunlight exposure and reduces shadows.

Raised bed installation helps improve drainage and avoid waterlogging problems. For easy maintenance and mobility between rows, think about adding paths. Additionally, arrange several geranium species strategically to avoid cross-contamination and promote well-organized record-keeping.

TOOLS AND EQUIPMENT

For efficient operations and productive cultivation, outfitting your geranium farm with the appropriate equipment and machinery is crucial. Daily maintenance operations like planting, weeding, and pruning require basic instruments like shovels, hoes, and pruners.

Geraniums prefer evenly moist soil, so invest in high-quality irrigation technology to provide regular and consistent watering. To keep the soil moist and keep weeds at bay, think about applying mulching materials. Larger farms can benefit from the use of mechanical equipment like cultivators and tractors, which can speed up some activities.

For equipment and instruments to last a long time and function at their best, regular maintenance is essential.

GETTING CUTTINGS OR SEEDS OF GERANIUMS

Establishing a successful farm requires choosing the correct source for geranium cuttings or seeds. Premium geranium cuttings or seeds can be obtained from trustworthy vendors, nurseries, or websites. Make sure the cultivar you select is appropriate for your soil type and climate.

Think about things like seedling vigor and germination rates if you're starting from seeds. Alternatively, if you're going to use cuttings, make sure they come from well-established plants, are healthy, and free of disease.

Building a partnership with a reliable supplier might be helpful for continuous production since a successful geranium farm depends on consistent quality. Maintain thorough documentation of your sources so you can monitor how various batches and types perform over time.

CHAPTER SIX

GROWING AND GATHERING

SOWING AND PROLIFERATION

A vital step in the cultivation process, planting signifies the start of a plant's life cycle. Appropriate planting procedures are critical to the success of horticulture. A farmer's cautious selection of seeds or seedlings depends on the particular crop they plan to cultivate. For the best possible development and use of resources, planting depth and spacing are essential.

The process by which a seed becomes a seedling is called germination. Sufficient soil conditions, temperature, and moisture levels are necessary for effective germination. To produce ideal conditions, farmers frequently use methods like presoaking seeds or employing germination trays. A high germination rate is ensured by keeping an eye on and changing these circumstances, which lays the groundwork for a robust crop.

CONTROLLING SOIL NUTRIENTS

For crops to develop and produce over time, soil nutrient management must be effective. Farmers use a variety of techniques, including cover crops, chemical fertilizer application, and organic amendments, to improve soil fertility.

A useful technique for determining nutrient levels is soil testing, which enables farmers to customize their nutrient management strategies to the particular requirements of the crop.

Plant health depends on a balanced diet, as excess or deficiency in any one nutrient can affect crop quality and output. Moreover, intercropping and crop rotation are used to control nitrogen levels and stop soil deterioration. Long-term productivity is promoted by sustainable techniques like organic farming and agroecology, which emphasize preserving soil health through natural processes.

TECHNIQUES FOR TRAINING AND PRUNING

Horticultural techniques like pruning and training help plants grow in ways that maximize yield, enhance quality, and make harvesting easier. To regulate the size and structure of a plant, pruning entails the deliberate removal of branches, shoots, or leaves.

This promotes better air circulation, focuses energy on fruit or flower development, and lowers susceptibility to illness.

Using support structures like trellises or pegs, training techniques are used to direct plant growth along a desired framework. This is especially crucial for crops that are vining, like grapes and tomatoes. Plants that are trained properly receive more sunlight, have better air circulation and are easier to harvest.

When combined with pruning, these methods improve the crop's general health and yield.

BEST HARVESTING PRACTICES

The process of harvesting marks the end of cultivation and the completion of all the work that goes into planting and caring for crops. Optimal methods for gathering crops differ according to the kind, but they usually entail choosing the ideal maturity stage, using the appropriate equipment, and taking caution when handling the harvested material.

Fruits and vegetables with the best possible flavor, texture, and nutritional value are those that are harvested on time. Harvesting crops with the right moisture content is essential for processing and storage, especially for grains and oilseeds. Cleaning, sorting, and packing are all part of the post-harvest handling process, which is necessary to preserve product quality and lower losses.

The best time to harvest generally requires farmers to weigh a variety of factors, including market demand, labor availability, and weather.

CHAPTER SEVEN

ASSURANCE AND QUALITY CONTROL

KEEPING AN EYE ON PLANT HEALTH

An essential component of quality control and assurance in agriculture is plant health monitoring. It entails the ongoing inspection and evaluation of crops to spot any indications of pests, illnesses, or dietary deficits.

Frequent monitoring makes it possible to identify problems early and take prompt action to stop the spread of illness and reduce yield losses. A variety of methods, including ocular examinations, sensor utilization, and data analytics, can be used to efficiently monitor the health of plants.

Farmers can enhance crop health and overall productivity by making well-informed decisions through the implementation of effective monitoring systems.

PUTTING QUALITY STANDARDS INTO PRACTICE

Putting quality standards into effect is essential to guaranteeing dependability and consistency in agricultural processes. Quality standards function as reference points for permissible limits of several aspects, such as crop quality, safety, and environmental sustainability. To satisfy legal requirements as well as customer expectations, farmers and agricultural practitioners are required to follow these criteria. Quality standards must be implemented by following specified growing procedures, using certified seeds and inputs, and adopting best practices. This boosts the overall sustainability and competitiveness of the agricultural industry in addition to improving the quality of the produce.

TECHNIQUES FOR MANAGING DISEASES AND PESTS

Techniques for managing pests and diseases are essential for preserving crop quality and yields. The goal of integrated pest management (IPM) techniques is to manage pests and diseases sustainably by combining biological, cultural, mechanical, and chemical control tactics. Common tactics include crop rotation, the introduction of natural predators for biological control, and the prudent use of insecticides. In addition to safeguarding crops, efficient pest and disease control also helps to minimize the negative effects of agriculture on the environment, support biodiversity, and guarantee the security of the food supply chain.

AFTER-HARVEST MANAGEMENT AND PRESERVATION

From farm to table, post-harvest handling and storage are essential steps in preserving the quality of agricultural products. The procedures that follow harvesting include washing, sorting, packing, and shipping. By following the right procedures after harvest, vegetables can be kept free from infection, deterioration, and physical harm, reaching consumers in perfect shape.

To extend the shelf life of perishable commodities, storage facilities with controlled environments—such as temperature and humidity control—are crucial. Using technology like cold chain management and refrigeration also improves the quality preservation during storage and transit. Reducing food waste and satisfying consumer expectations for fresh, premium produce are made possible by efficient post-harvest management.

CHAPTER EIGHT

STRATEGIES FOR MARKETING AND SALES

PUTTING YOUR PRODUCTS' BRANDING TO USE

Differentiation and customer recognition for your geranium products depend on building a distinctive brand. A strong brand includes your company's overall identity, core beliefs, and product promises in addition to your logo. Think about the special qualities and advantages your geranium items have to offer while branding them. Create a brand narrative that appeals to your target market and highlights geranium's healing and natural properties. Maintaining consistent branding across your products' packaging, marketing collateral, and web presence contributes to creating a unified and enduring impression.

CHANNELS FOR ONLINE AND OFFLINE MARKETING

Using a combination of online and offline channels is essential in today's ever-changing marketing landscape to reach a wide range of consumers. Social media, e-commerce sites, email campaigns, and other online marketing channels offer the chance to reach a worldwide audience and take advantage of digital trends.

In addition, offline channels that serve local markets and customers who desire in-person interactions include print media, events, and traditional retail locations. Maximizing visibility and engagement for your geranium goods through an integrated strategy that harmonizes both online and offline media enables a comprehensive reach.

DEVELOPING CONNECTIONS WITH RETAILERS

One of the most important strategies for growing the market for geranium goods is to work with merchants. Building trusting relationships with retailers requires listening well, figuring out what they need, and lending a hand when needed. Provide stores with instructional materials about geranium products so they can tell customers about their benefits. Promo assistance, prompt product deliveries, and flexible pricing are all essential elements in creating enduring partnerships. Establishing a rapport with merchants and keeping the lines of communication open can result in win-win situations that increase the exposure and sales of your geranium merchandise.

ESTABLISHING A SALES CHANNEL

To guide potential consumers through the purchasing process and turn leads into purchases, a clear sales funnel is crucial. Typically, the sales funnel is divided into phases like awareness, consideration, and decision.

Raising awareness in the context of geranium products entails focusing marketing efforts on the distinctive features of the items.

To assist customers in making educated judgments, the consideration step entails offering comprehensive information, client testimonials, and instructional content.

At last, the decision step concentrates on making the purchase easier through comfortable in-store experiences or smooth Internet transactions. Frequent analysis and sales funnel optimization provide a smooth and successful customer journey, increasing the likelihood that leads will become devoted buyers of your geranium goods.

CHAPTER NINE

MONEY HANDLING

FINANCIAL PLANNING AND BUDGETING

For any firm to have strong financial management, efficient budgeting, and financial planning are essential. In budgeting, resources are systematically assigned to different divisions, activities, or projects to the aims and objectives of the company. It acts as a road map, helping those in charge of budget allocation to allocate money in a way that supports strategic aims. Contrarily, financial planning takes a more comprehensive approach, taking into account risk management, contingency planning, and long-term financial goals.

In addition to aiding in cost control, a well-designed budget makes it easier to find possible areas for cost reduction and efficiency gains. It serves as a financial roadmap that facilitates the distribution of resources by painting a precise picture of expected revenue and projected costs. Beyond just creating a short-term budget, financial planning also includes risk management, liquidity, and overall financial sustainability plans.

STRATEGIES FOR PRICING

Pricing tactics are essential to a company's ability to make money. It takes careful consideration of several variables, such as manufacturing costs, market demand, competition, and perceived value, to determine the appropriate pricing for goods or services. Depending on their market positioning and commercial goals, organizations frequently use a variety of pricing techniques, such as cost-plus pricing, value-based pricing, penetration pricing, or skimming pricing.

In cost-plus pricing, the selling price is determined by marking up the production cost. Value-based pricing, on the other hand, takes into account how customers view the worth of the good or service. While skimming pricing includes setting higher prices early and progressively dropping them as competition develops, penetration pricing tries to capture market share by delivering products at cheaper rates initially. The organization's objectives and unique set of circumstances will determine which pricing plan is best.

ACCOUNTING AND MAINTAINING RECORDS

Accounting and record keeping are essential elements of financial management because they offer a methodical approach to monitoring, evaluating, and reporting financial activities. Decision-making, regulatory compliance, and stakeholder financial accountability all depend on accurate and current financial information. To create financial statements that show an organization's financial health, accounting entails the classification, measurement, and analysis of financial data.

Maintaining accurate records of financial transactions allows a company to keep an eye on its cash flow, assets, liabilities, and equity. Additionally, it makes preparing financial statements like cash flow, income, and balance sheets easier. Adoption of accounting standards and principles promotes financial reporting's uniformity and transparency and aids internal and external stakeholders' ability to make well-informed decisions.

GETTING GRANTS AND FUNDING

A crucial component of financial management is obtaining funds and grants, particularly for firms and nonprofits aiming to grow or start new projects.

Finding possible financial sources through grants, loans, or investors calls for a calculated strategy. When requesting financial support, organizations frequently have to make a strong argument that highlights their goals, mission, and expected outcomes of the money.

Nonprofits and specific projects frequently receive financial help from grants in particular. When submitting a grant application, an organization must carefully draft a proposal outlining its objectives, strategy, spending plan, and anticipated results. A grantor's priorities and the organization's mission must coincide for the acquisition of grants to be successful. Furthermore, organizations must implement strong financial management systems to guarantee openness and accountability. This will boost their credibility and increase the probability of obtaining funding.

CHAPTER TEN

GROWING YOUR BUSINESS USING GERANIUM

GROWING YOUR FARM

Growing your farm is a smart way to scale your geranium business, but it takes careful planning and execution. To ascertain the necessary extent of expansion, evaluate the market demand and your current production capacity. When choosing locations for new crop areas, take into account elements like the climate, soil quality, and resources that are available. One way to increase output while reducing environmental effects is to adopt sustainable farming techniques and install efficient irrigation systems. Investing in technology can also improve overall efficiency by streamlining processes and acquiring automated planting and harvesting equipment. To make sure that the expanded farm can satisfy rising demand and stay competitive in the market, it is imperative to carry out in-depth market research.

INCREASING PRODUCT VARIETY

A smart strategic strategy that can reduce risks and take advantage of new market trends is diversification. Go beyond growing geraniums and look for ways to expand your product offering. This can entail launching new geranium cultivars or expanding into complementary goods like potpourri, essential oils, and natural skincare products. To make sure that your varied offers meet market expectations, conduct a market study to determine consumer trends and preferences. Developing a reputation for excellence and innovation in your brand can attract a devoted following of clients. To ensure sustainable growth, it's crucial to carefully strike a balance between embracing diversity and keeping geraniums as the primary focus.

PARTNERSHIPS & COOPERATIONS

Establishing alliances and collaborations is essential to growing your geranium company. Form partnerships with distributors, retailers, and suppliers to expand your network and attract a wider range of clients. Forming alliances with academic institutions or agricultural specialists might give you access to important information and tools that can improve your farming methods.

To make use of shared resources and knowledge, think about establishing strategic alliances with businesses that complement each other in the perfumery or horticulture sectors. Co-branded goods and cooperative marketing initiatives can improve market presence and visibility even further. Developing solid connections inside the sector can lead to new business prospects and long-term success.

CONSIDERING THE INTERNATIONAL MARKET

To successfully expand into other markets, one must have a thorough awareness of worldwide trends, laws, and cultural quirks. To determine which target countries have a market for geranium products, conduct in-depth market research.

Think about forming strategic collaborations with companies that are already well-established in the target market or collaborating with regional distributors. To successfully enter a market, you must modify your products to match foreign standards and adhere to legal requirements. Additionally, while creating packaging and marketing methods that appeal to a variety of consumer bases, consider cultural variances. For effective distribution, establishing a worldwide supply chain and logistics network is essential. Keep yourself updated about geopolitical developments that could affect global trade, and be ready to modify your plan of action as necessary.

CHAPTER ELEVEN

ECOLOGICAL METHODS

ECO-FRIENDLY AGRICULTURE METHODS

Growing interest in environmentally friendly farming practices can be attributed to the agricultural sector's search for long-term answers to environmental issues. With a focus on soil, water, and biodiversity protection, these methods aim to reduce the ecological effect of farming operations.

Adopting organic farming practices, which discourage the use of artificial chemicals and encourage the use of natural fertilizers, is a crucial component of environmentally responsible farming. Agroecology concepts are also applied to improve biodiversity and establish a healthy environment on the farm. Crop rotation, cover crops, and integrated pest management are a few of the techniques that help make farming more sustainable overall.

PARTICIPATION IN THE COMMUNITY

One essential element of sustainable agriculture techniques is community engagement. It entails establishing a cooperative partnership between farmers and the neighborhood, acknowledging the connection between agricultural endeavors and the welfare of the community.

This interaction transcends the bounds of conventional farming and promotes candid dialogue, information exchange, and teamwork on initiatives that assist farmers and the community as a whole. Farmers' markets, community-supported agriculture (CSA) projects, and educational outreach activities are a few instances of how the community is involved in sustainable farming.

Locals can foster understanding, address issues, and work together to promote ecologically responsible farming methods by being involved in the farming process.

STANDARDS AND CERTIFICATIONS

Standards and certifications are essential for encouraging sustainability in the farming sector. Standards have been developed by several organizations and regulatory entities to evaluate and certify farms according to how well they follow sustainable practices.

Rainforest Alliance, Fair Trade, and USDA Organic are notable certifications. These certificates generate demand for sustainably produced items by reassuring consumers about the ethical and environmental methods used by the producers.

Adherence to these guidelines frequently necessitates thorough evaluations encompassing elements like soil conservation, water utilization, and equitable work methodologies. Farmers are encouraged to implement sustainable practices by certifications, which advances the field of environmentally and socially conscious agriculture as a whole.

SOCIAL DUTY IN THE PRODUCTION OF GERANIUMS

In geranium farming, social responsibility highlights the significance of just and moral business practices throughout the supply chain. This includes taking into account community development, fair salaries, and working conditions. Renowned for producing essential oils, geranium farming necessitates a delicate balance to guarantee that cultivation methods respect ethical norms and help nearby populations. Sustainable agricultural farming entails understanding the requirements of the local community, paying laborers fairly, and advancing the socioeconomic advancement of the area as a whole. Geranium farmers may strengthen their ties with the communities they serve by emphasizing social responsibility, which will help to create a feeling of shared accountability for the social and environmental effects of their farming practices.

CHAPTER TWELVE

PROBLEMS AND SOLUTIONS

TYPICAL OBSTACLES IN GERANIUM FARMING

Like any agricultural endeavor, geranium cultivation is not without its difficulties. An ongoing challenge for growers of geranium plants is their vulnerability to pests and illnesses. Aphids, whiteflies, powdery mildew, and bacterial leaf spot are just a few of the pests and diseases that these plants are vulnerable to. These problems might result in lower quality and productivity, which presents a big problem for farmers.

Growing geraniums presents additional difficulties because of the plant's sensitivity to the environment. For best growth, geraniums need a certain combination of moisture content and temperature. Geranium crops can be adversely affected by changes in weather patterns, unforeseen temperature extremes, or insufficient watering.

Farmers who want to sustain a steady and healthy crop must learn to manage these environmental conditions.

Furthermore, geranium producers face financial difficulties because of competition and changes in the market. Market developments and customer tastes may have an impact on the demand for geranium-related items, such as essential oils and decorative plants. Farmers' operations become even more difficult as a result of the need to diversify and alter their products to satisfy market needs due to this variability.

TECHNIQUES FOR SOLVING PROBLEMS

Proactive steps and reactive tactics must be used in tandem to address the issues facing geranium farming. To tackle insect and disease problems, integrated pest management (IPM) techniques can be utilized. To reduce the need for chemical pesticides, this entails combining biological controls, such as predatory insects, with cultural techniques, like crop rotation.

It is imperative to conduct routine crop monitoring to identify such issues in advance.

Farmers can make investments in climate-controlled greenhouses and other technologies to address environmental sensitivities. These structures make it possible to precisely regulate the light, humidity, and temperature—creating the perfect atmosphere for geranium growth. Furthermore, the implementation of effective irrigation systems, like drip irrigation, aids in the maintenance of constant moisture levels and the avoidance of stress caused by water.

When addressing economic difficulties, diversification emerges as a crucial tactic. Growers have the opportunity to experiment with various geranium cultivars, serve the needs of the essential oil and decorative markets, and participate in value-added activities like essential oil extraction through distillation. Developing trusting connections with customers and keeping up with industry developments can also help you adjust to the always-shifting market conditions.

GETTING KNOWLEDGE FROM FAILURES

Any agricultural enterprise is bound to experience setbacks, and geranium farming is no exception. Farmers must have a resilient mindset and see obstacles as chances for growth and learning when confronted with problems. Finding practical remedies begins with identifying the precise causes of a setback, be it a pest infestation or a decline in the market.

Regularly evaluating and recording the farm's performance might yield insightful information. To spot trends and possible correlations, farmers might maintain records of crop health, meteorological conditions, and market movements.

They can make well-informed decisions and put preventive measures in place to lessen the impact of setbacks in the future thanks to this data-driven strategy.

Within the farming community, cooperation is also beneficial. A culture of continual improvement is fostered through exchanging experiences and knowledge with researchers, agricultural specialists, and other farmers. Access to the most recent research and best practices can be facilitated by workshops, training courses, and agricultural extension services.

Growing geraniums has its share of difficulties, but growers can create robust and sustainable enterprises by using proactive problem-solving techniques and a dedication to learning from failures. Growing geraniums is a difficult industry, but farmers may manage the challenges it presents by adopting a continuous improvement mindset and approaching problems methodically.

www.ingramcontent.com/pod-product-compliance
Lightning Source LLC
Chambersburg PA
CBHW070818290526
45795CB00002B/756